From Mindfulness to love

Paul Bryden

From Mindfulness to love

By

Paul Bryden
(pauldbryden@gmail.com)

No part of this book may be reproduced in any form without written permission from the author. Permission is likely to be granted so please ask.

Copyright © 2015 Paul Bryden

All rights reserved.

ISBN-13: 978-1511659062
ISBN-10: 1511659068

From Mindfulness to love

My Brilliant Image

One day the sun admitted,
I am just a shadow.
I wish I could show you
The infinite Incandescence
That had cast my brilliant image!
—
I wish I could show you,
When you are lonely or in darkness,
The Astonishing Light
Of your own Being

Hafiz

This book is dedicated to everyone who finds life difficult

Introduction

This book is intended to serve as an introduction to Mindfulness and Meditation for someone who has no formal knowledge of either. I try to provide a flexible approach to allow the reader to gain some experience of Mindfulness, irrespective of their circumstances; for example, not everybody will wish to do a formal exercise like Meditation. I also encourage the reader to devise their own mindful practices to suit their particular interests and inclinations.

The title "From Mindfulness to Love" suggests, deliberately, that there is a journey involved - a journey which must pick up the threads of love along the way; they become inseparable and move ever onwards.

Mindfulness is very simple and most people will already have some experience of it in their own lives: this is where we start. I try to keep the guidance simple and focus more on the characteristics and feel of it, rather than on any rigid specifics.

Contents

Introduction 4

How to use this book 8

Mindfulness in brief 12

    First exercise 12

    Second exercise 12

    Third exercise 13

Mindfulness at length 15

    Who needs it? 15

    How to start 18

The Cognitive Approach 20

    The difficult things in our life. 20

    The pleasant things in our life. 21

    How the mind has developed to help us survive. 23

    Do we really have time? 25

What Mindfulness is… 28

    Our first experience 29

        First exercise 29

        Second exercise 30

        Third exercise 30

    The Body 32

Variations on our exercises 34

- Smell 34
- Taste 34
- Touch 35
- Sight 35
- Bodily Feelings 36
- The Characteristics of Mindfulness 37
- Where do these exercises lead? 39

Meditation 42
- Learning to meditate 43
- The meditation journey 47
  - Tranquillity 47
  - Insight 48
  - Thoughts as objects of concentration 51
- In the longer term 52

Back in everyday life 54
- Doing 'Chores' 54
- Try something new 54
- Human interaction 55
- Walking in nature 57
- Waiting 58
- Take moments 58
- Use cues to remind you to be mindful 59
- Do what comes naturally and easily to you 60

From Mindfulness to Love 61
- Patience 61
- Acceptance 62

From Mindfulness to love

Opening our heart 64

Love 65

Mindful Reminders 67

How to use this book

This book begins in three sections: a one line description, a short description and a longer description.

The one line description captures the essence of Mindfulness - it's a simple phrase surrounded by space ready for you to inhabit and interpret. Most people will want more instruction but, in the spirit of it, try and carry the implication of its simplicity with you as you (inevitably) move on to the short description.

As I said, Mindfulness really is very simple and I hope all of the important features are contained in the short description. Please try it and seriously consider it as being all you need to read. Of course you may feel a little cheated by the brevity, after all you'd settled down to read a book and perhaps you wanted a little more meat on the bones, or you don't believe it can be that simple – I mean...people do degrees in Mindfulness don't they? Can it be that easy? Well, yes.

The longer description is not long by the standards of a 'book' but it tries to describe why we might need Mindfulness, and to anticipate the questions and pitfalls you might encounter. The problem I have with it is that, in a sense, it's just feeding the problem you have already recognised you have; a brain that is too busy. It took me many hours to write, but I would be very pleased if you never read it and instead spent the time *actually being* mindful, discovering for yourself all the ways of bringing Mindfulness into your life and enjoying the effect it has on you day to day. Mindfulness is an experience, not a teaching. The usefulness of any teaching is to guide you to the experience. That said, you might wish to know about the Mindfulness in the wider context and be aware of some of the ideas around it. Some people will prefer the extra guidance in the longer version. I concede the suggestion that you 'go and be mindful' will not work for everyone - a lot of people are more confident when they feel that they are working with something with which they have thorough conceptual grasp. If you already realise that's you then by all means skip the short version and go straight to the longer one. Alternatively, you may just want to read the short one and then dip in to the longer version and use it like a handbook.

After those descriptions of Mindfulness you will find: an introduction to Meditation, 'Back in everyday life' and 'From Mindfulness to love'.

I'd like you to read the meditation section. Meditation is not essential to Mindfulness, but it is very helpful. The snag for many is that it can be quite difficult to find a time and place to do it, but it's worth it because the depth of the experience it brings has the potential to unlock a lot of our inner world.

The 'back in everyday life' section discusses our application of Mindfulness to the way we live and the effect it has on us. It might help you find ways of discovering mindful experiences outside of any formal exercise like Meditation.

'From Mindfulness to love' is very much about the extended mindful journey, so don't be in a rush to read it. Slip it into your luggage for now and take it out when you wake up somewhere wondering if this is where you're supposed to be.

At the very end there are some 'Mindful reminders' – bullet point ideas for being more mindful in your life.

Lastly, I would say that in most cases attending a class in Mindfulness is better than reading a book.

From Mindfulness to love

'Mindfulness is about simply being,

rather than thinking about being'

Mindfulness in brief

Sometimes when we are doing something very simple, walking in the country, or engaged happily in some task of no great consequence, a warm, relaxed mood can come over us and for a few moments we are not thinking of the past or future but are completely absorbed by the present and we feel content. If you have ever felt like that you will have had a moment of Mindfulness. Alas, typically our lives tend away from such moments, rather than towards them, as we are drawn into the rush of it all. Before long it seems that we are caught up in a downhill rollercoaster of demands and thoughts with no brake. My aim here is to help you to regain those spacious moments and find a brake to the onslaught of thoughts. Mindfulness isn't about thinking, it's about doing (or being), so let's do something, now:

First exercise

At the end of this sentence put down this text and listen to the world around you for a minute or so.

You probably found yourself identifying the sounds you heard and then drifting off into stories and thoughts related to them or something else entirely. Let's try it again, differently.

Second exercise

This time repeat the exercise and try to drop the stories and implications. At first allow yourself to isolate each sound, but then see if you can start to hear all of the sounds together – closer to the way you might listen to music; approach it as an orchestra of sound. At the end of this sentence put down this text and listen for a minute or so to the world around you in this revised way.

That will have been more difficult. In between the odd moments of success there were probably periods of self doubt about "this is silly" or "oh darn I'm isolating things again". This is a first important lesson in mindful activity – don't beat yourself up when you find your mind drifting off, instead congratulate yourself for noticing and go back to it; noticing your thoughts is an important part of Mindfulness. Now we'll add some more to it:

Third exercise

Adjust your posture to one that says 'relaxed' eg uncross your legs, allow your arms to rest on your lap or a table top. Allow your shoulders and chest to relax with a couple of deep breaths and then start to pay attention to each breath. Breathe in a natural, unforced way and become conscious of the air entering and leaving the body. Then start listening to that 'orchestra' of sound again. Hear all the sounds interplaying and shifting. Try not to identify sounds or their sources or judge them. At the end of this sentence put down this text and breathe and listen for as long as you wish (you might get to like it!).

Did you find that easier? This exercise introduced some very important aspects to Mindfulness: We have to enter it with the correct intent and that can be developed by some brief preparation, also it introduced the importance of the body as a partner to the mind. If we relax the body the mind will follow. So often we can get away with just 'going through the motions' with an exercise, but Mindfulness isn't like that. We have to absorb ourselves in it. In many ways that absorption is what Mindfulness is. Now how did you feel at the end of the third exercise? What I'm hoping you felt was a spaciousness, a feeling of relaxing into the body, a few minutes rest from the chattering mind and a just a hint of contented wellbeing.

In the third exercise we use the breath and hearing as objects of concentration, but we can use any of the senses as objects of concentration, individually or in combination. We don't have to be sat quietly either - we could be walking or doing some gentle exercise like Yoga or Tai Chi. Try eating mindfully – concentrating on the taste and texture of the food. Walk in nature and be absorbed by the smells, sounds and the rhythm of your steps. Do gardening mindfully; how does the soil feel and smell? Be in a queue mindfully, don't be impatient, instead enjoy the breath and any sounds or views. Find mindful ways of doing the 'chores' in your life.

Here are the key points about being mindful:

- Arrive at the exercise with intent and an awareness of the body.
- Allow one or more senses to absorb your concentration.
- Gently drop any thoughts as soon as you notice them.
- Enjoy the feeling of wellness that develops.

Outside of the exercise we could add 'observe how it improves your life'.

Now go and be mindful, find ways to let it seep into your everyday life. Try to unlearn the imperative of continually doing things. Humans need reflective space – the brain uses that time for valuable creative and constructive ends that will benefit you.

Give yourself permission not to have to achieve anything for a short time everyday and do a regular Mindfulness exercise - learning meditation is ideal; there are instructions later in this book.

If you are too busy then make friends with time again by spending more time in the present. Give it the chance to make you content.

Mindfulness at length

'Mindfulness is about simply being, rather than thinking about being'

In other words it's about the experience of life in the moment, as delivered by our senses, rather than what we think our life is, as delivered by the stories, fears and fantasies of our mind.

Maybe for people who aren't mindful, it's more easily described by what it isn't, and what it isn't, is those incessant thoughts about what might be, or might have been. It may seem like that's all we are: one thought after another, in a frenzy that never stops, even when we are asleep, but that isn't necessarily the case. Thoughts can stop, and when they do stop what you are left with is what your senses are delivering to you about the world in that moment. Our problem is this: thoughts are compelling to the extent that we often make the assumption that we *are* our thoughts. It's much more helpful to see thoughts as just things that happen to us.

Who needs it?

There are those who would say we all need Mindfulness, but I am not sure that's true. I'm quite happy with the idea that there are plenty of people who lead well balanced, stable and fulfilled lives without any training in Mindfulness. Life is about meaning, or a search for it, and it's typical of human arrogance that we suppose our meaning is better than someone else's. I think if we could see into the minds of others we would be amazed at how different the world seems from within that mind. Language and culture restrict our interpretation and reporting of our world, so that our actual experience of it is highly filtered when we attempt to describe it to others and that can preserve an illusion of similarity. The implication for Mindfulness is that we all come to it with very different beginnings: some people just don't need Mindfulness, some people have always had it, some people learned it naturally, and some of us only find it by being taught it. This book is for those of us who have to be taught it.

You probably know people who don't need Mindfulness, maybe someone you have always admired for their poise and clarity and ability to cope in all situations. Alternatively, there are those who have rejected the mainstream world for a simpler life; artists, or people who live close to the land, people who have instinctively engineered their lives to be more conducive to their good health. They may not call it Mindfulness. They may just call it giving themselves space, or living in harmony with nature but, regardless, they have found a natural way of incorporating it into their lives. This route may not suit all of us; for whatever reason we may have to exist at the 'bleeding edge' of life and, within those constraints, maybe we have begun to recognise the need to search for something that will reduce the worst effects of living that way.

It's worth remembering that not everyone who needs to be taught Mindfulness needs it because their minds are filled by the relentless activity of our working, family and social lives. Some people may lead a comparatively inactive life, but still their heads are full of sadness or anxiety and they need to learn techniques to reduce that burden. These are typically the people I have been teaching Mindfulness to in classes; people whose mental functions have become challenging enough for them to have difficulty in coping with a normal life. There may be a rhythm to their illness - ups and downs that are seasonal, regular or irregular, or related to medication regimes. For these people the way to approach Mindfulness is to learn the technique during the healthy phases, the times when there is good motivation and concentration, which will then help them through the worst of the difficult phases. During periods of poor concentration, low motivation or other mood extremes, it is unlikely that useful learning progress will be made from a book. In less extreme cases the extra absorption a class offers may just work.

If you fall in the 'busy' category, the bad news is that Mindfulness takes up time – it has to, that's kind of in the definition. So if you really are cramming sixty one seconds into every minute something is going to have to give. But the good news here is that you probably aren't using your time as efficiently as you thought you were. Mindfulness exercises can take up the slack time while we are travelling, or every time we are stood waiting for something – those moments that your busy mind thought were 'wasted' because all it could see was that nothing productive was getting done. In modern times, these are often the moments we reach for our mobile phones. But from a different mindset something more useful can be done – instead of sitting impatiently during this 'wasted time' we could be doing a Mindfulness exercise that reduces our ambient stress levels, better prepares us for our next activity and makes waiting a more pleasant experience – a triple whammy of usefulness! But there is also a sense in which Mindfulness gets us back some time. As our experience of ourselves becomes more objective and honest we discover how many of our 'essential' activities we actually added to our lives in order to distract us from how difficult our lives had become. Amongst these are our uses of drugs, food, sex, exercise, shopping and socialising or social media, all of which could have a role in a healthy life, but all too easily can be used as diversionary activities to help us forget our dissatisfaction. As we become more aware of ourselves we learn to weed out the unhealthy aspects of these activities and leave the essential ones, giving us more time for new interests and Mindfulness exercises such as meditation. The problem with explaining it that way is that it rather puts the cart before the horse, because we need to make the investment of time first, in order to get it back when we discover which habits we can most usefully drop. So, for the time being at least, something has to give in order to find time for mindful exercises. That might be a difficult message at first, but it will pay off later.

How to start

A pitfall which can beset people on the mindful road (and self-helpers generally) is the tendency to make Mindfulness another 'activity'; instead of the *inactivity* which is intended. What I mean by this is we can get caught up in 'learning' this new thing and wanting to read (and buy – the shopping impulse!) more books on the subject. You really don't need to. Mindfulness is very simple - that's why this book is brief. The message here is not to be active and acquire knowledge, but instead to start *unlearning* things - to unlearn the compulsion to be busy and to unlearn our bad diversionary habits. We don't need to become a Mindfulness expert; just be more mindful. If you are an intelligent and active person you are at a disadvantage here, because you are used to solving problems by thinking about them. With Mindfulness the opposite is true – we are going to solve problems by *not* thinking about them. Instead, we are going to change our relationship to them.

So...when you read this book I'd like you to put it down a lot.

If you read a section that speaks to you, that you suddenly identify with, or register as true to your life, pause a little and give yourself space to absorb that moment. There's no need to rush on to the next sentence – it will still be there later! Make reading this book your first exercise in the real life application of Mindfulness. I ask you to start with that now, because I am at a disadvantage in delivering these ideas to you in a book because I can only deliver cerebral concepts and the real lesson in Mindfulness, the one that will stay with you and bring you back to it, is the experiential lesson. I can implore you to look for that experience, but I can't give it to you, I can only suggest where and how you find it and maybe describe what it feels like so that you recognise it. That's the strength of going to a Mindfulness class - I still couldn't actually deliver the experience, but I could set up all the conditions to bring about the experience – it would be a step closer.

Before we get on to what Mindfulness is in more detail, I just want to indulge in some very unmindful reflections about our thoughts, because a large part of what Mindfulness is about is developing a freedom from them; recognising that our thoughts are just things that happen to us and that we can choose to ignore them if we wish. Developing an objectivity, a distance from our thoughts, is a very important part of the process. That objectivity begins with starting to recognise the kind of thoughts we are having and asking ourselves whether they are as useful to us as we had assumed.

The Cognitive Approach.

This is a discussion about what we spend our time thinking about, why we think it and why we have lost the ability to simply enjoy the pleasure of the 'now'.

The difficult things in our life.

Whether it is the conversation which we just left, or some dark episode from our childhood, it is often the difficult things in our life that are the source of our most compelling thoughts. These thoughts from our past are often marked out by a sense of something unresolved or unfinished in our life, or simply not understood. The more distant of these leave bad feelings or atmospheres, which, although they are too obscure to yield specific thoughts, they nevertheless colour the way we think and react in certain situations in our life. As the recollections get more recent they are associated with specific stories we tell ourselves again and again, in the hope that some new understanding will arise, but it never does and we just reinforce the habit of the story telling. We become locked in loops of injustice or bewilderment. We don't move on, because there is no new information to lead to any new conclusion; it just festers, and with each re-telling the feelings return from the original situation. With those feelings our internal chemical armoury repeats its reaction and our muscles tense and our heart beats faster – a damaging and useless response to an event that, otherwise, would just be history. It serves no purpose - there really is no point to re-examining anything that happened in our past life beyond the first few recollections, unless we have new information about it. If we could have worked it out we already would have done.

Similarly compelling are the worries for the future. Our anxieties about what *might* happen can consume us to the point where we try and plan against and anticipate all eventualities. Since the possibilities are infinite, it can be a never-ending exercise. As a result, we can excessively try to control our lives in order to protect ourselves. This can add to our anxiety when life defies our control and we worry, not just about the outcome, but also about the failure of our control. A certain amount of anticipation is useful and essential in modern life, but so is the ability to respond creatively and spontaneously to how our life unfolds. Indeed, that's probably a better skill than trying to control every aspect of our lives. Again, in the absence of new data, a few iterations around how a given future might play out will serve as useful preparation; beyond that it is needless worry.

As long as we are locked into concerns about the difficulties of the past and future we are not in the present and so are ignoring the possibilities of the present, namely that it may be a calm and pleasant place to dwell, and resting there can prepare us for confronting the real problems of life in a composed and relaxed way.

The pleasant things in our life.

It may be a surprising thing to say, but what I'm about to imply is that thinking about the nice things in life is not always helpful either, because it detracts from our actual enjoyment of life. Again, the past and the future can conspire to steal us away from our present.

Some of us, especially as we get older or experience difficult times, can reach into memories of the past as somewhere that was 'better' than now, for example when our partner was alive, or reflecting on the simplicity of childhood. Some elderly people can be examples of this, their lives may have contracted to a series of a few, very predictable, events and their memories, aided by the array of photographs on the shelf, are endlessly re-told, often with the difficult bits omitted, as balm to relieve the perceived tedium of the present. It would surely be better to have a real, vibrant, present to live within?

For others of us the hoped-for pleasures of the future probably predominate in our pleasant thoughts. For the sick there is the perpetual hope that the future will provide some relief from our discomfort. There is no harm in wanting a better life, but there is also some value in admitting that, at this moment, life is painful. This is a difficult step, but acceptance always leads to less suffering, eventually. This needs more explanation and I will come back to it.

What about those of us who are not ill? Well, consider for a moment how we look forward to the end of the working day, to the weekend, or to our holidays, for relief from our working plight (if we have a moment!). And, if we're lucky enough to enjoy our jobs, by which I mean we savour each moment we are able to work in them, do we not still indulge in moments of fantasy about how life might be? These might be fantasies about romance, about achieving success and adulation, about sexual conquests, or winning a race or contest - we all have such fantasies, but what good do they do? Why is it somehow preferred to sit and fantasise rather than to stop thinking and merely enjoy the present where we are (probably) warm, fed, in no great pain and, hopefully, excited by all the possibilities being alive has to offer? These pleasant thoughts, although not reinforcing negative emotions, are still a kind of diversionary escapism that are no substitute for accepting the real experience of being alive and part of the living world, as opposed to the *thought* world.

I am not saying you shouldn't reflect on the past or consider the future, but I am asking you to start to notice how often you do it and then to ask yourself what you think it's achieving? I am suggesting that most of us have got the balance wrong and we need to shift that balance away from reflection and anticipation and towards spaciousness and listening to a different internal world, the world of the senses and feelings. I suspect you already agree that less reflection and anticipation would be useful, but are maybe less convinced about the value of senses and feelings. That's OK at this point - their value is only likely to be understood by experience and I will attempt to justify them later in the book.

So, those above, are some of the ways in which we are drawn away from the experiences of the moment, but why have we lost our interest in our experience of now? Why is now somehow less compelling than our thoughts of the past and future?

How the mind has developed to help us survive.

The complete title for this might be 'How the mind has developed to help us survive *at the expense of allowing us to just to be.*'

As we develop as children we have to learn to process the sensory information from the world around us in the most efficient way possible. We cannot accept the vast amount of information from the senses without some short cuts to its significance, otherwise we would be constantly overloaded and confused by it (like in autism, maybe?). To avoid this happening, the brain lumps together a group of sensory experiences and labels them for future use. So, instead of re-learning 'a chair' every time we see or feel one, we draw on a template that says 'chair' whenever our sensory impressions are close to a certain pattern and thereafter we just call up our assumptions about a chair without having to work anything out: It is flat, stable, has four legs, is designed for us to sit on etc. Our entire world is built in that way during childhood; when children sit mesmerised by some very simple object that is what they are doing – cataloguing the building blocks of their world, in order to improve the speed at which they can respond to it in future. But once we have done that with the key features of our familiar environment we assume there is no benefit from further examination. We stop being inquisitive about them until someone points out some new feature, or new use for an object and instead we hurriedly move on to gather more of our world. We eventually write things off as 'understood' and then we stop experiencing them with any depth.

Witness, for example, how we will photograph with interest the features of a new town in some unfamiliar part of the world while we are on holiday, but completely ignore our home town. Yet a local from the holiday town might do the reverse. There is little that is intrinsically interesting or boring about most towns. That quality is brought by how we see it, the 'eye of the beholder'. Typically our mature interest is only piqued by the unfamiliar, the novel.

So when we say be mindful of what is around you, of what your senses are telling you about this moment, we are asking you to go beyond the template, to rediscover the childhood fascination with the apparently simple, to re-engage with the world. Our reluctance to do that is because our brain does not see the point – and it does require a little effort to work against this instinct.

Having catalogued the world in this way the brain is then free to get on with the important job of survival. The child has grown up, and now its interest in the static world of objects is increasingly replaced by interest in the dynamics of the world, a level of sophistication not possible so long as it was bogged down by understanding the fundamental building blocks. Now its priority is with the more complex interactions of objects. Does this person threaten me or my family? Is my status in the tribe being challenged? Was that moving object something I can catch and eat? Can I mate with him/her? I'm using these primitive examples because that's the stage to which the brain has evolved; it hasn't caught up with modern life. You might argue that learning Mindfulness is helping us to compensate for that.

As young adults not only have we lost interest in the simple, but we have also gained a new restlessness, we are constantly on our guard for outward stimuli that offer threats or opportunities. Far from dwelling on the simple and restful, we have now acquired an imperative for our distraction – our survival may depend on it.

These two qualities of the developed mind, our cataloguing and our restlessness, work against our Mindfulness. Consequently most of our work in our mindful exercises is aimed at un-learning these, or perhaps we should say re-learning the qualities of simple interest and concentration.

Do we really have time?

While we are discussing the cognitive, I want briefly to try to undermine our assumptions about what time is, or, at least, illustrate that there are other ways of looking at time, and to suggest our accepted western approach is only one of them. I do this because our sense of time is also germane to why we find being mindful difficult; we feel that time marches on and leaves behind those who do not march with it. We are locked into a work ethic and culture that values time above all else and we often feel guilty if we are not using every moment of it 'productively'. Our assumptions about time imbue it with the high value we put against things that, once lost, can not be regained.

The hands of a clock may travel at a constant speed, but our impression is not necessarily of an evenly moving time. It depends on what we are doing; it is subjective. More than that though, I want to challenge our cultural assumptions about time and introduce the idea that other cultures (never mind species) do not share those assumptions. As I said at the beginning, "Language and culture restrict our interpretation and reporting of our world". The language of a culture gives clues about how its people understand and interpret the world. How that relates to time is explained here by someone who says it better than I could:

"In the 1930s a man named Benjamin Lee Whorf began to clarify an insight he had had into the structure of the Hopi language. Hopi has only limited tenses, noted Whorf, makes no reference to time as an entity distinct from space, and, though relatively poor in nouns, is rich in verbs. It is a language that projects a world of movement and changing relationships, a continuous "fabric" of time and space. It is better suited than the English language to describing quantum mechanics. English

*divides time into linear segments by making use of many tenses. It is a noun-rich, verb-poor tongue that contrasts fixed space with a flow of time. It is a language of static space, more suited, say, to architectural description. All else being equal, a Hopi child would have little difficulty comprehending the theory of relativity in his own language, while an American child could more easily master history. A Hopi would be confounded by the idea that time flowed from the past into the present."
Barry Lopez – Arctic Dreams.*

Indo-European languages commonly describe time by using the concepts of space e.g. 'the future is ahead', 'the past is behind'. The South American Aymara language reverses this concept by seeing the future as 'behind' and the past as 'in front', an idea we find challenging.

So it's true to say that time exists, but our view of it is not the absolute we pretend. It is a human construct. We invented it to serve us but, as is so often the case with unchallenged human inventions, *we* increasingly serve *it*. If we are to be more mindful we are, to some extent, going to have to embrace a 'less is more' world which challenges the dominion of time over our lives by questioning whether time is finite or serial. We often talk about giving ourselves 'space' in this context – a term for a vacant part of the third dimension. Interestingly we have no equivalent word for the forth dimension - it doesn't fit our cultural model, the best we have is 'pause', which implies it starts again, just where it left off.

But now let's draw a line under all these cognitive considerations, because it's not the important bit. Our brain may enjoy the cerebral exercise but it does not get us any closer to where Mindfulness dwells. In human culture the domain of Mindfulness is in nature, art and in the dissolving human boundaries that yield empathy, compassion and love. But, before that even, in ourselves, its realm is sensory. It's in the immediate experiences of our life, so that's the direction in which our enquiry now needs to move.

I'm going to quote Barry Lopez again to illustrate what I mean. I think the following says much the same as the previous quote, but in a very, very different way:

[He's been camping out watching birds for several days.....]

"The night I thought I heard rain and fell asleep again to the cries of snow geese, I also heard the sound of their night flying, a great hammering of the air overhead, a wild creaking of wings. These primitive sounds made the Klamath Basin seem oddly untenanted, the ancestral ground of animals, reclaimed by them each year. In a few days at the periphery of the flocks of geese, however, I did not feel like an interloper. I felt a calmness birds can bring to people; and, quieted, I sensed here the outlines of the oldest mysteries: the nature and extent of space, the fall of light from the heavens, the pooling of time in the present, as if it were water." Barry Lopez – Arctic Dreams

I am just trying to introduce the idea that time may not be what it seems. It may be that by approaching our lives in a certain way we can slow it down and expand sections of it, create puddles of time we can play in, before we step back into the place of clocks.

What Mindfulness is...

We have seen in the earlier sections how the restless mind likes to distract us away from the present and into a world of its own making; the stories about how life was or might be. This is where it wants us to linger – all the things Mindfulness isn't! The mindful alternative is to bring our attention where life *is*; our moment by moment experience of the world as delivered to us by our senses. It can be an everyday (every minute, even) exercise in taking the time to experience the details of the things around and within us and how they change moment to moment; a single thing or the complexity and interaction of many things. Instead, now, as we study these details, we ignore the temptation to be drawn into the stories, the understandings, the explanations for what we experience and we just stay with the qualities of the experience.

This is unlikely this is new to you. Almost all of us will have experienced it at sometime, to some degree. In everyday life Mindfulness is an open fire on a winter's day; allowing the warmth, the colours, the crackles and the smells to engage our senses, but not thinking "I need to buy more logs", or "I remember my dad teaching me to make fires". It could also be lying on a beach on holiday, feeling the heat of the sun, the feel and smell of the breeze, the sounds of the waves and of children, the patterns in the sand - but resisting the thoughts of how long you can reasonably leave before you go for your next ice cream (I'm found out...!).

It can also be that moment when some unknown impulse makes you stop between activities and a subtle sense of wonder and contentment creeps over you. You find yourself staring at some simple phenomenon, a passing cloud or swaying tree and, for that moment, everything just seems right – as if it could be no better. Have you had that? Some do, some don't, but that might simply be because we all have differing habits and would benefit from a few simple exercises and prompts to make mindful experiences a more common part of our lives.

Learning Mindfulness is not necessarily about learning something new, it's about being introduced to ideas and exercises that make Mindfulness something that can be summoned at will, instead of just happening in ideal or chance situations, and hence be made to happen more often and occur more naturally in our lives.

In the next section I will build up to a mindful experience in three exercises in order to demonstrate some of the important qualities of Mindfulness.

Our first experience

Here are a series of exercises for people who are new to Mindfulness. They are a series of very simple steps designed to help home in on what Mindfulness is and how it differs from our 'normal' interface with the world around us. We are going to concentrate here chiefly with the sense of hearing. It could be done with the other senses but, because each sense has its own unique quality (a fascinating subject in itself), the guidance would be different.

First exercise

At the end of this sentence put down this text and listen to the world around you for a minute or so.

If we examine what happened my guess is you heard a series of things, in the room, outside and maybe even within yourself (tinnitus, for example) and that you tended to identify each one, scanning around them, 'ticking them off' against the catalogue we discussed in 'How the mind has developed..'. You may also have noticed yourself drift off into the stories and implications around the sounds e.g. "I can hear the gutter dripping, I must get that repaired" This is our normal approach to the world around us – we question 'what do I need to know about this in order to survive well?'

Second exercise

This time repeat the exercise and try to drop the stories and implications. At first allow yourself to isolate each sound, but then see if you can start to hear all of the sounds together – closer to the way you might listen to music (unless you're a musician – they might be quite analytic); approach it as an orchestra of sound. At the end of this sentence put down this text and listen for a minute or so to the world around you in this revised way.

That will have been more difficult. In between the odd moments of success there were probably periods of self doubt about "this is silly" or "oh darn I'm isolating things again". This is a first important lesson in mindful activity – don't beat yourself up when you find you're mind drifting off, instead congratulate yourself for noticing and go back to it. I'm not just saying 'congratulate yourself' to put a positive spin on things – you have witnessed you own thinking and made steps to alter it – that's a Mindfulness fundamental! The next exercise is similar but with an added activity I hope makes the 'orchestral listening' easier.

Third exercise

Adjust your posture to one that says 'relaxed' e.g. uncross your legs, allow your arms to rest on your lap or a table top, lie down if you wish. Allow your shoulders and chest to relax with a couple of deep breaths and then start to pay attention to each breath. Breathe in a natural, unforced way and become conscious of the air entering and leaving the body. Then start listening to that 'orchestra' of sound again. Hear all the sounds interplaying and shifting. Try not to identify sounds or their sources or judge them. At the end of this sentence put down this text and breathe and listen for as long as you wish (you might get to like it!).

Did you find that easier? Just giving the brain that extra bit of activity, ironically, helps our restless mind to settle. This exercise also introduces two other important aspects of Mindfulness: we have to enter it with the correct intent, which can be developed by some brief preparation, it also introduced the importance of the body as a partner to the mind, that if we relax the body, the mind will follow.

When we think of some of the exercises we've done in our life many of them have not really required any element of engagement with the process behind them. For example doing push ups will increase your upper body strength, irrespective of what attitude you are bringing to it, and even mental exercises like learning times tables still work even if you're actually focused on what you're about to have for lunch. True enough, they would benefit from engagement, but many of us got by without it! It's not so with Mindfulness. In many ways the engagement, the absorption into what we are doing, *is* the Mindfulness. That's why the intent, supported by the preparation, is so vital. You have to want to do it and you have to be prepared to clear everything else out of the way for it. Doing it in a perfunctory way, just going through the motions, will not work. We have to take a little time to set ourselves up - and the body can be of great help in that.

Now how did you feel at the end of the third exercise? What I'm hoping you felt was a spaciousness, a relaxing of the body, a few minutes rest from the chattering mind and a contentment. For me this has a place in the body. I feel as if something inside my chest is slowly slipping lower and opening up in the space behind it is a fuzzy glow. I'm not saying it has to be this way for you, but my point is this is a pleasant experience – similar to a feeling of homecoming – recognising a place to relax into. So I hope you felt something like that, however subtle. But there may have been other things there as well, little twinges of something like sadness or elation, or excitement, or anxiety; just hinted at, hidden away somewhere.

You may not have noticed them yet, but they are part of the natural background of feelings. They are the things we often don't notice while we are going about our busy lives, but in this more attentive state we glimpse them 'in the wings', waiting to tell us important things about ourselves. We'll come back to them later.

If you felt the third exercise wasn't convincing, maybe it's worth doing it again having read the last couple of paragraphs. Also be relaxed about it, not obsessive about getting everything right. Be playful and curious, not demanding. It also may be that my choice of using hearing and the breath is not a good one for you. Often the way into Mindfulness will vary between people, depending on the relationship they have with their various senses. A musician will hear differently, an artist will see differently, someone who has panic attacks or asthma will have a different relationship to observing their breath. Later on I will introduce some more ideas around different senses ('Variations on our exercises'). Try some of those if you have difficulty with the third exercise.

The Body

In the modern west there is little recognition of a body-mind connection. This is less so in the east where, in some traditions, they barely make any distinction between mind and body. For that reason, when techniques like Mindfulness are brought from the east to the west they need some translation into a culture that treats body and mind as separate. The following is written in recognition of that.

In our perception of ourselves I think most of us will recognise that the body and mind will often exert an influence over each other, where one tends to mimic the experience of the other. For example, if the body is ill the mind will experience distraction and discomfort (e.g. depression, shock) and if the mind is ill the body will often exhibit symptoms too (the psychosomatic, nervous habits). Luckily this works *for* us as well as *against* us. We can influence the mind by mirroring the desired response in the body. If we want to relax a busy mind then inducing calm in the body is a good start and that's what we were doing as we began the third exercise. This is also why Yoga, Tai Chi and other physical exercises are great partners to Mindfulness and meditation and, if approached correctly, *are* mindful or meditative in themselves. This is not just saying the body can help Mindfulness - that would be to understate the connection - Mindfulness can barely exist without the sensory feedback of the body. When earlier I described witnessing our thinking as being a Mindfulness fundamental, it is equally true to say that witnessing our body is a Mindfulness fundamental.

There are parallels also with the mind and body's healing process. Imagine you have damaged your finger. We instinctively want to bend the finger as part of our normal handling of things, so we start to train our mind not to bend the finger, otherwise it will hurt. We also understand that the best thing for a damaged finger is rest, because we know our body mends itself if we don't meddle with it too much. But we typically do the opposite with our mind. If the mind is troubled by something we endlessly re-visit the pain and actually give it less rest. Mindfulness is saying do the reverse; treat the mind like you would the body, bring your awareness to it and rest it.

Variations on our exercises

For most people it is the third of our three earlier exercises that will have given them the authentic mindful experience – it had all the right components. (If you had success in the earlier two you probably don't need this book!) I'd now like to expand on that last exercise, substituting different senses, because it's important to illustrate that any sense could be used. Some people may find one of the others works better for them than hearing. In our expanding experience of Mindfulness it is also important to look for new sources of mindful experience, because this is going to help us incorporate it into our daily lives. When trying out the rest of these senses ease yourself into them the way we did with exercise three; bringing intent and preparation with appropriate breath and posture.

Smell

Repeat the third exercise substituting smell for sound – smell relies on the breath so they are natural partners. Those of you with good 'noses' will again be tempted to isolate out individual smells, try to avoid that and move away from judgements of 'good smell' or 'bad smell'. This exercise works best away from your natural environment, where you have probably 'normalised out' the smells around you. It's a good thing to try on a walk in the country, for instance.

Taste

Like smell, taste often requires a little outside stimulus to work well as an exercise, so try it when you next eat. Try the breath too, but this also works well in combination with touch as we examine the texture of the food we are eating. Eat slowly and allow the tastes to combine and alter as the digestive process begins, also feel the changing textures and tastes as the food is chewed. For people like me who tend to eat too quickly this is very good for the digestion, but not so great if you're eating with other people who aren't being so mindful and they want to clear away the dishes!

Touch

Repeat the third exercise substituting touch for sound. The easiest way to do this is to pick an object up and roll it around in your hands. Close your eyes and, again, don't get caught up in the labelling of 'hard' 'soft' 'cold' 'bumpy' etc. but let the feeling be more like a massage of your hands *by* the object as it moves across them. Of course you could also just use your two hands feeling each other, or another part of your body. You can try doing this when you wash or shower, or do the washing up with the feel of the soapy dishes. (The Mindfulness of washing up is perhaps the most well known example of Mindfulness put into domestic practice, as suggested by Thich Nhat Hanh.)

Typically, we are not aware of our clothing against our skin, or the sensory information our muscles are delivering about posture or the points where our body is being supported by the ground or chair - but these are all potential sources of felt bodily information we can use. Our posture and points of support are often used within a 'grounding exercise' in preparation for Mindfulness and other therapies - like we did in the third exercise. Touch also works well with the breath, and if we focus on the feeling of the breath on the skin around the nostrils, the two experiences almost merge.

Sight

This is surprisingly difficult and best done with the breath. Sight is a very restless process. Normally we are not aware of the eye continually scanning objects, but once we start to pay attention to that process it can become distracting. The best approach is to slightly defocus like we do when we 'stare into space' or to watch something that is itself in slight motion, like a candle, or the clouds, or branches swaying.

Bodily Feelings

I mean here the inner feelings of the body, irrespective of whether we attribute them to physical or emotional sources. The most important of all of these is the feeling of the breath as the body expands and contracts with our inhale/exhale cycles. The breath can be used alone or in conjunction with other senses to great effect and probably is the most useful mindful resource we possess.

When I attempted to describe the feeling in my body as a result of exercise three I was a referring to a type of bodily feeling which is closely connected to the emotions and to wellbeing. There are many more such feelings that most of us are familiar with, for example associated with nervousness or happiness, and then there are those more subtle feelings that we may only begin to see as we practise Mindfulness. We must also mention the aches and pains of the body.

Bodily feelings are a very separate group which, excepting the breath, may not be of immediate use to the beginner but become more important as we become more adept, and can be used as an object of concentration like the other senses. Often one of the reasons we need Mindfulness is because we are actually subconsciously creating a busy mind in order to avoid recognising a particular feeling. As we become more mindful we create the space and calm that gives us the resources to turn towards difficult feelings, instead of away from them, which eventually helps us to release our emotional past (see 'Insight').

If you have a problem using the breath because you find the breath an uncomfortable object of concentration I have two suggestions:

Firstly, take your awareness away from the chest, lungs, throat and down towards the belly. Feel the rise and fall of the belly as the air enters and leaves the body and use each cycle to push your awareness lower towards the pelvic floor. Think of the belly moving not as the breath itself but something which just happens as a consequence of it and allow its subtle movement to become the object of concentration.

Alternatively, you could shift your awareness even lower in the body to the points of contact with the floor or chair. Sense that through these you are rooted to the earth and supported by it, feel a heaviness and a drawing of all energy low into the body and through that into the ground.

(These can also be quite helpful when we have excess energy. They can be used separately, or together, as 'grounding' techniques.)

The Characteristics of Mindfulness

These simple mindful exercises are typical of many that we can introduce into our lives quite easily when the opportunity arises. Mindfulness can also take on other different, more formal, activities like meditation, Tai Chi, yoga, chanting or walking, which outwardly seem quite diverse in that some are physically active and others aren't, but the common quality is the end effect they are having on the mind in the short and longer term. Hopefully, you now have a personal experience of that short term effect. I want to take some time to uncover the common thread in all these activities to give you more confidence in finding your own route to a mindful end, because we shouldn't limit our activities to those we are taught. Some people will be successful with a prescriptive approach which details what to do, others of might enjoy the discovery of a new approach based on their own preferences and fuelled by their curiosity. In many ways the last, more creative, approach is better, because it will keep our practice fresh and more engaged.

The goal is to quieten the mind and, as I've outlined above, that is unlikely to happen if we are allowing it to roam into the territory of the past or future. Instead we anchor it to the experiences of the present and the only experiences we have that do that reliably are the senses. Typically this will be the breath or other bodily feelings, but it can also be sight and sound (and others, but they're rarer as practices). I talk about quietening the mind and not stilling the mind, because it is usually a progressive process. The mind does not want to stop, so usually a better approach is to give the mind something very simple to do, often a repetitive physical action, and then concentrate on how that feels within the body, for example in meditation, where we commonly use the breath as the object of concentration. The simple motions of Tai Chi and yoga (once learned) provide just enough stimuli for the mind to work with that it ceases to crave the additional activity we are typically used to and so can be effective mindful exercises. The caveats to this are that, while learning these techniques, mindful experience might be illusive if we are worrying about whether we are getting our technique right or not. Also there is no reason to suppose they will be taught as mindful exercises. They can be taught very unmindfully but might still be correct to their tradition, so the reader will have to bring their own interpretation to the exercises. The lesson here is that any simple physical activity can be approached in a mindful way if the goal and method are understood. The method is that there should be very little thought or calculation needed, such that we become absorbed into the bodily feeling of the activity, and we should not let the mind drift off into distracted thought. That probably rules out competitive sports, unless they can be done by instinct rather than calculation. The goal is to arrive at that relaxed, spacious space where we are content and focussed. Walking is good example and has the added benefit, if we are walking in nature, that our other senses are also stimulated by the environment around us, so we can have that ensemble effect of being absorbed by the entirety of our sensory apparatus.

So, there are many approaches to Mindfulness and your approach will depend firstly on what works for you and secondly on what opportunities for Mindfulness arise in your life. I would always encourage some form of regular formal exercise, daily if possible, in association with any number of shorter opportunistic exercises based around your natural activities. By formal I mean activities like meditation, Yoga or Tai Chi, appropriately taught, or modified. It doesn't really matter what activities we employ - you could even make them up - as long as we recognise they have the characteristics of Mindfulness, which are:

- We arrive at the exercise with intent and an awareness of the body.
- We allow one or more senses to absorb our concentration.
- We drop any thoughts as soon as we notice them.
- We steer some of our concentration towards the feeling of wellness that develops.

The last point deserves some elaboration, because we haven't discussed it yet. As our mindful experience deepens we find, associated with the successful absorption into the object(s) of concentration, that feeling of wellbeing I mentioned. It helps if we then incorporate that bodily feeling into our objects of concentration, partially shifting towards it, whilst still aware of the others. As long as we don't shift all our attention towards the feeling it will act as a feedback mechanism to keep us on track. We also do this because it's something to recognise and enjoy. We should avoid shifting all our attention to it though, it can be too distracting.

Where do these exercises lead?

Although Mindfulness may be practised regularly in whatever formal exercises we choose (e.g. meditation), our aim is to make Mindfulness an instinctive and integrated part of the activities of our lives and, through that, to improve our lives. We are looking to turn these mindful exercises, which might now seem a little staged and disconnected from real life, into exercises that form part of our normal everyday activities. To do this we can use the example of our taught exercises and apply our interpretation and intelligence to re-invent them around how we live. In an ideal world this would be so deeply ingrained that we could drop the formal exercises altogether, but in my experience few people achieve this. So, in part, our intention here is to remind ourselves continuously about that experience of contentment and quiet that is just a small step away from wherever we are, no matter how stressed. This is very consoling and can be a great resource to our lives, but this spaciousness has other uses as well, apart from lowering our anxiety.

In "the cognitive approach" I hope I gave some insight into the way in which we constantly turn to our thoughts and how unhelpful some of those thinking habits are. Having been made aware that 'our thoughts are not us' introduces the idea that we can step back and witness our thoughts without being committed to them or controlled by them. We gain objectivity to our thoughts and behaviours. This is another value to the spaciousness of Mindfulness – the space it gives us can be used to enhance this objectivity. The more it comes into our lives, the more we start to see our behaviour critically and dispassionately, and the more we begin to be less reactive to situations and more considered. We also question our own motives and begin to see the extent to which our thoughts and actions are driven by underlying feelings and emotions. We don't always do things for 'thought out' reasons. Often in difficult situations what happens is: we feel, we act, and then we think. In such cases thoughts can come in retrospect as a justification for an action that was prompted solely by a feeling. Furthermore we may have had little impression of that feeling and no understanding of it in its own right. Mindfulness creates the objectivity that allows us to unfold and separate these events and it helps us to understand ourselves more deeply. We can learn to ask how we feel, examine what we think, and then act.

Another vital aspect to Mindfulness, and the way it influences our approach to our life, is that we learn to be more tolerant of the things we judge as unpleasant. These may be external to us, like a noise, or internal like an emotion, or physical discomfort. Our typical reaction to something unpleasant is an internal, bodily felt, stress caused by our rejection of the experience. That added stress is unnecessary. Mindfulness suggests that we shouldn't reject whatever is unpleasant. Instead, we allow it to be, take an interest in it, stop labelling it as 'unpleasant' and regard it as just another sensation. This has great implications to our approach to pain, depression and anxiety – all conditions that, by not being mindful, we make worse by our reaction to them.

Mindfulness is about changing our habits. The more we practise coming back to the present, then the more we reinforce that habit and the more natural it becomes to have that new awareness in our life. It's about unlearning the habitual thoughts that get us nowhere, learning the habit of coming back to our experience of the present through our senses, and then using that enhanced understanding of what's going on in our lives to make better decisions and focus on the things that are most important to us. In business jargon it results in a reallocation of resources.

All through our life we have layered our experiences, one on top of another, and it matters how neatly each layer is put down. Events that were difficult will not lie evenly and, like layers of sheets carelessly shoved into a linen cupboard, the creases and lumps will show through the layers right to the top, to the present day. They do not lie evenly because we were not sufficiently resourced to deal with them neatly as they occurred, perhaps because we were too young, or too stressed. Mindfulness gives us the space to 'iron out' each layer before the next is laid so we no longer need to add to the confusion of contours in our emotional landscape. Further to that, as we will see when we come to talk about Insight meditation practice, we even have a tool which helps us go back and re-bed some of the earlier layers.

Meditation

The word meditation comes with baggage, especially if you are not a meditator, but even for those who *are* there's often a suspicion that it should be something more than what you are experiencing! It is not about sitting in lotus position, it is not about being more 'spiritual' and it is not about achieving amazing psychic states, or blissful experiences. It may be any or all of these, but we should not expect it to be because to *expect* meditation to be anything would be taking us away from the experience of the present and that would not be mindful. Meditation is Mindfulness in its most concentrated and pure form, usually reduced to one object of concentration done at length in an environment where distraction is minimised. Just bear in mind it's taught in many different styles and I am only going to introduce you to one of these.

Our consideration of Mindfulness so far has been about a practice done more in the outer world, the world we live within. Meditation shifts that emphasis to the inner world, the world which lives within us. I say 'shifts the emphasis' because to work within one is not necessarily to exclude the other.

Where our Mindfulness exercises may use the breath and hearing or other senses, meditation only uses one of these to start with, typically the breath. The strength of our mindful exercise was that it could be done anywhere, but I'm going to suggest that meditation is best done in a quiet room with few distractions. Our mindful exercise had no duration set against it, because using time opportunistically was rather the point, but meditation is best given a formal duration. How long to set aside for meditation is a regular enquiry from students and there is no good answer. The best answer I ever heard is:

"40 minutes is about right, unless you are very busy and don't have time, in which case maybe you should do 60 minutes" (I got that from Peter Mallard at 'The Barn', who got it from someone else.)

The point is it depends on your circumstances - if you come to it with a settled mind 30 minutes may be enough. But if you come to it with a busy mind you may indeed need 60 minutes, which emphasises that preparation (and intent) is all. Personally, I do it for 30/40 minutes after a similar period of yoga first thing every morning. Choosing the right time in the day is often crucial – finding a combination of when your mind is quiet, but not sleepy - but also when your house is quiet too. I recognise that for some people that combination is impossible. My best suggestion then is to find a meditation group nearby. That helps with the problem of a noisy house and also adds to the potency of the activity, which is helpful on those occasions when your attention is otherwise flagging.

The role of music in meditation is one which deserves comment. Some people who come to meditation assume, because of the wide availability of 'music for meditation' that it is necessary component, but it isn't. In fact I would discourage its use. That's not to say it should never be used; for some people the soothing and entrancing qualities of music help draw them to a peace they would not be able to achieve any other way – and who could deny them that? But once you are confident in the meditation process and, if not too distracted by noises of your environment, it is worth dropping the use of music. The reason is because the full riches of meditation are only felt when we become completely absorbed in the realms of *our own* experience, whereas to listen to music is to, in effect, be influenced by someone else. I think this will become clearer in the sections about Tranquillity and Insight.

Learning to meditate

'When we say we are going to meditate we are giving ourselves permission not to have to achieve anything for the period we have set aside.'

I think this describes meditation in our busy world. We might feel a kind of guilt about just doing nothing for 30 minutes but if we call it 'meditation' then that's OK. However you justify it is fine; it's recognising the need and then doing it that matters. Reading that definition you might say "but surely we're trying to *achieve* meditation?" ...sort of, but be wary of now bringing that same work ethic (the one whose permission we needed) into the meditation itself. Meditation is a 'less is more' thing; we can try too hard and demand too much. With that in mind, let's look at the stages of meditation:

Meditation is a Mindfulness exercise so our four bullet points, used previously, still apply:

We arrive at the exercise with intent and an awareness of the body.

We begin meditation by arriving at it with intent and an awareness of the body. We are conscious that we have set aside this time for meditation and that above all other things this is what we want to do. This is important. If you are really burning to do something else you should recognise that. What often helps as part of the preparation process is to formalise it: prepare the room, the light, the cushions in a considered (Mindful!) way respectful to the process. Then settle into your meditation posture with the same care. We're going to place our body in a sitting position that says to the mind 'alert' rather than 'relaxed', so maybe sit in a dining or office chair with feet flat on the floor and arms resting on the lap. To give the 'alert' message sit with a straight back with shoulders back, rather than slumped forward; to do that it may help to support the arms so they are higher. Our pose is 'Alert', but not too stiff – we're going to have to hold this for 40mins or so. The head is best held looking slightly downwards and eyes are closed, or open with a soft gaze. These instructions are just guidance – discover the needs of your own body. Once settled into position, take a few deep breaths and use the outbreath to drive your awareness deeper and lower into the body.

We allow one or more senses to absorb our concentration.

Be aware also of the way the body is supported and held, perhaps notice the sounds that are present within and outside the room and the how the day is outside - the temperature, light and weather. We are trying to make a smooth transition here, and to acknowledge the outer world we are ever in relation to, before we shift to our inner world. Then bring the awareness back to just the breath entering and leaving the body. We are going to focus solely on the experience of the breath and its cycle now: To do this examine the passage of the breath through the nostrils, nose, back of the throat and chest, but also witness the motion of the whole upper body from the belly to the shoulders. As you do this pick one place where you are going to focus your concentration, then use that place for the duration of the meditation. It is important not to influence the breath as we observe it. It should be a natural breath. There is no intention to make it slower, or deeper, or even more regular; it should just be whatever the body needs it to be. Try and get engaged with the breath, with the whole of its cycle, not just the in/out, but through the turning point as the in-breath seamlessly becomes the out-breath, and so on. Become absorbed and fascinated by the simple act of breathing.

We drop any thoughts as soon as we notice them.

As we allow the breath to flow and we try to hold our attention on it we will inevitably drift off into thoughts because, as we discussed earlier, this is what the brain is designed to do. The only important thing is that we notice that process happening and reverse it and come back to the breath. We must not get impatient with ourselves. If we must judge then we can congratulate ourselves for noticing. If the thoughts become too intrusive, we can remind ourselves of our intent and of the blessed relief of not needing to consider anything but the breath. A successful meditator is not one who has no thoughts, but one who has not taken the thoughts anywhere; a subject arose, but it did not become a story. It's rather like the difference between a word and a sentence. A word is a fragmented idea, a sentence gives the idea life. If we capture a thought in the present we have no more than a concept, if we give that thought a past or a future then it becomes a story, and demands our attention. Often in meditation we use the image of thoughts passing like clouds across the sky. Indeed every sensation can be seen as passing in the same way, whether thoughts, sounds, or discomfort.

We steer some of our concentration towards the feeling of wellness that develops

Slowly it becomes easier to follow the breath and ignore the thoughts and in response to that increase in concentration a softness seeps into the body, as if a space is opening up inside that is just a little warmer and more content than we are used to. This is subtle feeling, but recognising it is useful because we can include it in our awareness as useful feedback, although to concentrate on it too strongly might be distracting. We can learn from the yoga practice of 'breathing into' a feeling – combining attention on the breath and the feeling with each cycle.

The ending of a meditation session should be formalised too. Meditation is often best done to a set time, rather than to our own impression of time and so it's useful to use a timer to help with any anxiety about practicalities like 'is it time to get the train yet?' There are some good phone apps designed for meditators but any (quiet!) alarm would do. Give yourself time at the end of a session to have a stretch, re-arrange the room and re-enter the day. Too much activity immediately after meditation can be a bit jarring so try and slip gently into it.

This is essentially all meditation is. You might even be disappointed to hear this - after all what about all the amazing experiences people report that I alluded to earlier? As far as Mindfulness is concerned whether they happen or not is beside the point. The reason we do meditation in a mindful context is to help train the mind to turn away from thoughts whenever we wish and to observe the sense of wellbeing and relaxation that happens as a result. We keep practising this so the brain becomes trained to settle in a calm place, rather than an unhappy, worried or anxious place. It's a re-wiring of the brain - exploiting the brain's 'neuroplasticity', in jargon terms. But let's say a little more about the potential of meditation and the two types that are relevant to us, which are called Tranquillity and Insight.

The meditation journey

Tranquillity

Part of what meditation offers is the promise of tranquillity. If we know nothing else about it we probably carry that one impression, and it is the quality that is most relevant to Mindfulness. As a consequence, we often come to meditation with a desire for an escape from our current experience into this tranquil place of peace and of comfort. In some ways we come to it seeking something similar to the diversionary activity of shopping, or drinking, but we recognise the need for something healthier and less damaging, and meditation fits the bill. Meditation does deliver this tranquillity but, as we begin to realise the limitations of treating it as an escape, it can also start to offer the healing we actually need.

The tranquillity comes in several ways:

The mere act of regular deep relaxation lowers our background stress and makes us more resilient to stressful situations because we meet them from a place of greater composure.

Another sense in which tranquillity is gained happens over time as we deepen our practice and we push through to places of stillness that are quite new to us. These are often associated with very pleasurable sensations. These feelings are quite inspiring but, if we are not careful, we can find ourselves too obsessed by them and can too easily make these the goal of meditation. They are not the goal, nor are they the measure of 'a good meditation', they are just things that happen sometimes. By all means enjoy them, but don't go looking for them next time. Meditation is about opening our heart to whatever experience is there in the moment, it's not about expecting something to happen.

We also gain tranquillity by losing some of the stresses that our own psychology has brought to bear on us. These are the hang ups and foibles we have had for most of our adult life, which make us react to simple life events in ways that are disproportionate, or emotionally inappropriate. If you don't recognise these in yourself then you are either very lucky or you're about to have an interesting learning experience!

The limitation of seeking the escape I mentioned is that we often see the escape we need as being from difficult events outside of ourselves. Undeniably this could be so, but often a new objectivity tells us that the problem was actually within ourselves. It was our reaction to events that made them seem difficult, not the events themselves. As a consequence, no matter where we run to, the problems always catch up with us. We find it is not the world which needs to change, but ourselves. So, although Meditation may seem like an escape for a while, we find, as we get proficient at it, that it becomes more like looking at ourselves in a very honest mirror. It offers us the extra objectivity to ourselves that is necessary to see ourselves more clearly. It shows us what wants to change, and that is the biggest step toward change actually happening. These changes are not strictly part of Mindfulness in the sense in which it has been re-invented by Western practices, but it is an inevitable consequence of progress through Meditation, so it needs to be discussed.

Insight

Meditation can just be about nurturing tranquillity, but there is another element which I have variously described as 'change in ourselves', or 'healing'. I'm introducing it now using the more widely used term 'Insight'. When we sit in meditation and open our heart to whatever experience is there, in the moment, it is inevitable that, as well as thoughts arising pertaining to our life situation, emotions will also arise. Amongst these are the some of the 'subtle bodily feelings' I referred to back when I was discussing the use of the various senses in Mindfulness. They can occur during meditation because we have dropped the distraction mechanisms which we may well have been using to divert our attention away from them. Fear of such feelings may make you see this as a problem with meditation, but it is far from that; it is a consequence of a new honesty about our experience. It gives our feelings a chance to tell us things about ourselves that we have ignored for too long, and it gives the potential for their resolution.

If we come to such a moment in meditation it may manifest itself in many ways. It may have the hallmark of an emotion and be felt, for example, as an anxiety, or as nausea but it could also exhibit itself in many ways such as discomfort, irritability, or feeling too hot. The important thing is to turn towards such things in meditation; not to turn away from them in the way we may be inclined to do in everyday life. As we sense the emergence of a feeling we turn towards it, bring it into our awareness and we witness its qualities, without thinking about it, or judging it. This can be tricky at first, but with time we get better at it.

This, then, is an exception we make to the usual Mindfulness rule that says that we stay with the object of concentration and don't allow ourselves to be deflected from it. In this case we are going to incorporate the feeling into the object of concentration (the breath) in a similar way to how we incorporated the feeling that arose as we start to achieve a certain level of concentration and stillness. You recall we do this by 'breathing into' the feeling, by imagining that the breath is bringing energy to, or from, the feeling on each breath and we emphasise whichever we perceive it needs. It is largely our choice to take this direction and we do it because we came to Mindfulness to improve our life and, instrumental to improving our life, is the deepening of our relationship with ourselves and our needs. This happens more easily as we embrace more of our inner world and gather more of the lost corners of our psyche together and regard them with interest and kindness, rather than rejecting them with fear and hostility. The feelings we so often reject carry with them many of the solutions we seek.

This style of meditation is often called 'Insight' meditation because of the way it gives us insight into our own psyche (and also, in Buddhist terms, insight into the spiritual realm beyond our selves). It is not really a separate meditation to tranquillity meditation because, in our meditation session, we will typically start developing tranquillity and then move to the insight practice as suggested by our experience and/or inclination. It is usually our choice to move to insight work and it will happen once we feel we have sufficient resources of stillness and confidence built up in the tranquillity phase of the session. When we do it it'll be because we're OK with doing it and it feels right, not because we feel we 'should' do it for some reason, or that it 'ought' to be the next step.

Sometimes insight work is like sitting with a feeling and keeping it company, as if we are getting to know it and feel comfortable with it. If it alters in any way we follow its changes with curiosity and kindness. Come to the feeling with all the qualities you would give to a shy animal or hurt child. Occasionally the feeling will transform and reveal itself, which can be quite emotional and tears may flow, but they are not the sad tears we are used to; they are more like tears of understanding and of rediscovered love. A good deal of the composure we associate with regular meditators comes, not so much from the regular journeys into the tranquil realms, but because they found this way of crying and of healing themselves.

You may feel this talk about 'transformation' and 'crying' is all a bit scary and is not what you wanted from meditation. That's fine, you don't have to go there. Certainly try and gain some months of meditation experience before you make any conscious steps towards Insight work. In mentioning it here I'm preparing you for the longer journey, one you may have no intention of taking just now, but, in time, who knows? As I said earlier it's not, strictly, part of Mindfulness training, but it's a great opportunity for discovery. Remember also that, in order to prepare you, I have just discussed the difficult experiences; there are also many that are beautiful and enlightening that you won't need help with.

In the above I am implying that we have the choice about whether to stay with tranquillity meditation or whether to move on to insight work, but it's not quite that clear cut in my experience. We will always start with some tranquillity work because access to effective Insight work only happens after some settling of the mind. Beyond that we can influence the move to insight meditation, but sometimes it will just go there as part of the natural unfolding process of meditation. I would always say go with it. The mind/body will take us there when it knows we are ready for it; in fact that's the best way to discover it.

When we engage with a feeling in insight work it is the beginning of a process of resolution that has its own timescale. Although things might complete within a meditation session, they may also extend beyond and resolve in another session, in dreams, or in a quiet moment in our life. Rarely, this may result in us leaving a meditation feeling more uneasy than when we started, but we have to trust that the process will complete when appropriate. There is a tendency with meditation teachers to ignore this possibility but, in my view, it is a natural consequence of bringing that new honesty to our experience of ourselves that, now and again, we might be left feeling a little raw or exposed.

Thoughts as objects of concentration

It is my hope that by the time you have arrived here in this book you will have gained some understanding of Mindfulness for yourself and have tried meditation. I'd like now to add another object of concentration that may have been confusing had I introduced it earlier, namely thoughts. ("What?" I hear you say...) Now obviously I don't mean that we use a train of thought as an object, that would be to contradict all I have said, but I talked earlier about the difference between a word and a sentence: that a word could hold a concept or idea, but the sentence gave it a story, a life. The type of thought I'm suggesting here is the conceptual thought; the 'word'. I want you to be sure that when we say that a train of thought is discouraged (the sentence) we are not discouraging conceptual thought (the word) because these can be very helpful in Insight work.

Conceptual thoughts have their roots in the same place as feelings – in the subconscious, and they have the same potential to guide us closer to our internal world (rather like dreams). They come from an intuitive place that influences us constantly, but defies our control or interrogation. In meditation it is important to give them their space, not to force a story on them, but allow them a little room in which to manoeuvre and shift, often in association with a feeling. They may, literally, take on the form of a word, or it may be an image, or an idea that defies such definitions, but the key is to allow them to exist in a simple way, without letting the mind run riot with their possible implications. These conceptual thoughts, although not common, are very valuable and are at the roots of our creativity and our sense of discovery.

In the longer term

Alas, meditation is not like learning a sport in that you don't just keep getting better at it the longer you do it. That may be your initial experience over the first year or two, and this can be a very fruitful period, but eventually I think most meditators have a stale period where 'nothing much happens', or that is our perception. It's useful then to try something intensive like a retreat in order to become re-engaged with the practice. Almost any meditation retreat would probably do, but one teaching a different style might also help stimulate a renewed interest. Or try a regular class, if only so the teacher can re-assure you 'yes, that's normal!' In my experience (21 years) meditation rarely becomes easy; there is always effort involved in doing something that is going against the interest of the ego, which is the source of a lot of our thoughts.

Before we leave this introduction to meditation I want to re-state something I only alluded to earlier:

Don't meditate to improve your meditation, meditate to improve your life.

Meditation is not an end in itself. The measure of its success is not in having 'amazing' meditations, it's in noticing your life is getting easier. You are more content and better prepared for the things that crop up. You are less anxious about the future and life has become more enjoyable.

This has just been an introduction to meditation – it can be a big subject and there are many versions of meditation. There are books which will discuss all its aspects at greater length, but it's probably better just to do it for now and then ask someone, or read a book, if you come across problems. There are many experienced meditators out there who would be only too pleased to help you, if asked.

There are also variants on how to approach the 'Mindfulness of breathing' method I describe above. These use counting, or acknowledgements, of each breath, which some people find helpful.

Back in everyday life

Let's now look in more detail at how what we have learned in Mindfulness might influence our everyday life.

Earlier we did our three exercises and then looked at how they might be modified to include each of the senses, sometimes alone and sometimes in combination. I also talked about how we can expand those exercises and incorporate them into our daily routine. So now let's look at some ideas about how to do that.

Doing 'Chores'

Try and bring a new dimension to some of the existing 'chores' in your life. I mentioned washing up earlier, but it is equally applicable to cleaning the house, doing the ironing, or doing the gardening. See if you can approach them with less of an agenda or schedule. If you have half an hour spare and the ironing needs doing, don't set the goal that all the ironing has to be done in that time, just allow it to happen without expectation. Make your priority the experience of ironing; the motion of the iron, the smell, the way the body moves and the folding of the clothes. Most chores will benefit from being treated in this way. Some people enjoy these tasks by bringing these qualities to them and they never had to be taught. I confess I still don't relish them, so I can't promise that, but they no longer *add* to my stress like they once did. The habits we bring to our lives are deeply ingrained!

Try something new

Consider adding new activities into your life that have a naturally mindful association. Learn a craft or an artistic skill for example. Watch out for the pressure not to 'fail', or the competitive pressure to better others if you're in a class. Try to drop the idea that your works will be judged by anyone else. If necessary do them alone and tell yourself you will discard them afterwards. Looking to the future to how they will be received by others is not to be mindful of what we are doing. Do the activities for the sake of doing them. Enjoy and absorb yourself in the process of creativity. Tell yourself you are not doing this to produce a 'good' result but to learn more about the medium and the creative process, give yourself the freedom to make mistakes in order to learn from them.

Artistic activity is a great way of incorporating the sense of sight into our Mindfulness. If we draw something, for instance, we will immediately find we are challenging the assumptions our brain made when we 'catalogued' it early in our life. We realise it is more varied and nuanced than we ever assumed it was. Ninety percent of art is seeing, the rest is the manual skill. In learning a visual art we are learning to see in a new way and unlearning our crude assumptions about what was there.

Human interaction

Mindfulness has great implications for our interactions with other people. Having conversations mindfully, by which I mean listening to people mindfully, is the first thing we can work on.

So often in a conversation, instead of listening to the other person, we use that time to anticipate where they are taking the conversation, to judge that direction and to prepare our response. To listen mindfully is not to anticipate or plan but to open our ears (and our hearts) to what they have to say and allow them to be heard in their entirety without (our) distractions. We catalogue people, especially those we know well and love, in the same way we catalogue things and we make assumptions and projections about their intent. By the same process we also tend to trap people at a certain point in their evolution as people and don't allow them to change or develop by denying their changes. This may stifle them and damage our relationship with them. Listening mindfully to those around us can have massive implications, being fully heard by someone should not be the rare privilege it typically is. Try to recollect the last time you felt truly listened to by someone – it was probably quite an emotional conversation. To be a mindful listener we make sacrifices. We give up the option of giving a 'smart' answer at the end. We have to drop any agenda we had when we came to the conversation, and we are less likely to get our way at the end of it. We are also giving the person free reign to speak at length and tell us things we may not want to hear. It's difficult, but the reward is a new honesty in the relationship, a chance to truly understand instead of assume, and the opportunity for both parties to grow. All too often we only have ears for our own preconceptions. Having listened mindfully we will find a time when it feels right for us to speak. When we do speak our words may be less persuasive, but they will be more honest and more likely to be heard in the way we would wish.

This is not about listening mindfully to the sound of their voice in the way we approached hearing before. Indeed it's less about hearing than feeling. As you listen, witness your own feelings in response to what they say. Allow yourself to be moved and carried by their words. Allow your empathy to flow in response. Notice the way the mind wants to jump in and add responses, to defend itself, to extrapolate, to add your own story or understanding - and then try to ignore those urges. Drop the need to store up responses until it's 'your turn'. Instead allow the speaker to continue with your full attention. Unfortunately the less you know someone, the easier this is, so strangers are often a good place to start. I am lucky - I have a voluntary role that is really just about listening to people at their bedside. Sometimes people, often near the end of their life, will allow their story to flow, there is nothing to hide anymore and nothing to protect from a stranger, so they talk and I just listen. Their eyes are as open as a child's and my heart opens more with each sentence and it feels like the greatest privilege to be sat there needing to bring nothing to this conversation other than to listen, and believe, and love. It repeatedly reminds me of how rewarding just listening can be.

Walking in nature

This is perhaps (for me at least) the great 'ensemble' Mindfulness experience, where all the senses come together and feed into a single moment. The mere experience of being outside can re-affirm our relationship with the world around us as we start to sense the temperature, the smell and feel of the air, the quality of light and the sounds around us. Our animal heritage wants us to pay attention to these things. We may have forgotten why, and we might not consciously draw any conclusions from them, but this imperative to our lives is still recognised somewhere within. This helps us to bring our awareness to nature without effort. As we move within nature we add to the mix the awareness of our walking and breathing and the associated motions of the body and, not least, the sense of how we feel in response to this... Elated? Awed? Apprehensive? Nature is the perfect accompaniment to Mindfulness because we immediately feel small within it yet part of a greater whole and that helps us to get ourselves in perspective and aids our objectivity to ourselves and our problems.

Even quite a busy brain can be mindful in nature, because there is so much detail in which to involve itself. That's OK, as long as we don't get drawn into the thoughts of naming the bird, or reading the map, or questioning the why's and wherefores. The perfect response to the part of us that wants to question and enquire is to acknowledge our sense of awe and intrigue at the vast complexity of nature, but not take it any further. Just to rest with how wonderful and perfect it all is. The busy brain will also like the way it can drift from sense to sense and object to object. Normally we would be cautious about this in Mindfulness but my experience is it works fine in nature. We soon find our pace slows and our mind with it. Again it's about bringing the right attitude to our practice; we should try to drop expectations in terms of time, or event, or even destination and just do a little aimless wandering in some corner of the world that has been patiently waiting for the chance to captivate us.

Waiting

Our world increasingly demands immediacy. When we want something we want it now, so when we have to wait we can be very impatient. Impatience does not serve us well. The big things in life typically come slowly and, if we are not good at waiting, we look for short cuts and second best options. Worse than that it makes us unhappy and irritable and we take that out on ourselves and others. Mindfulness offers us a solution for the immediate, short term events and that has the possibility of helping us with the bigger, longer term things of life.

When we are forced to wait for something we first should recognise our impatience building. We might be looking around or doing some displacement activity like tapping our fingers. When you notice this (or before!) try coming back to the breath and shift your body awareness lower in your torso. Perhaps begin to scan the senses for any interesting object to focus on – maybe, if stuck in traffic, the feel of the steering wheel or the view out of a window. Deflect the mind away from considerations of time. Ask if the deadline you're setting yourself is actually important, maybe it isn't? There may also be the sense that this delay has got in the way of what you had intended doing – but does that really matter? Whether we are stuck in traffic, queuing in a shop, or in the doctor's waiting room, try not to use that time to fret, or fiddle with a mobile phone. Use it to relax and come to terms with waiting. This training of the mind makes waiting more pleasurable. It will be useful later on in difficult life situations like separation, illness and other life events that take time and over which we have no control. Waiting patiently will also mean we approach our next task in a better frame of mind. Patience is one of the first, and most valuable, lessons Mindfulness brings.

Take moments

There may be odd mindful moments you can grab between activities like moving between rooms, rearranging a workspace or waiting for a colleague. You might also deliberately put a pause in what you are doing, if only for a few seconds, and bring some simple exercises to these moments.

Try these; you can pretty much continue them in the order given depending upon how much time you have.

- Come back to the simplicity of feeling the breath enter and leave the body.
- Take your awareness lower into the body following it shift down through the torso.
- Ask yourself 'how do I feel right now?' and feel the response in the body.
- Ask yourself if anything, in this moment, is actually wrong? Look for what's good about now.

Use cues to remind you to be mindful

Some people are helped by setting up reminders to be mindful. These can be an alarm on a mobile phone, watch or computer which reminds you to take a moment out from whatever you are doing to do a short exercise like that above. They can also be in the form of visual prompts like a sticky note placed somewhere it's frequently seen. Or you might use a regular event, like opening a door, or climbing stairs as a prompt to be mindful.

Coping with difficult emotions

For some of us emotions such as fear, depression or anger may have been a difficult aspect to our lives with the power to suddenly overtake us and dictate our actions. Under such influences it can feel like we are at risk of losing control, which is frightening in itself. In the section on Insight Meditiation we discussed how to approach feelings within meditation; that instead of turning away from them we sit with them and breathe into them. As we become more proficient we can bring what we learn in meditation into everyday life and treat these difficult emotions in the same way. By learning to 'be with' these emotions we cease to be frightened by them and remove the power we had been giving them.

It takes a little time and practice to get to the stage of being able to erode this fear but it is a very useful application of what we learn in meditation and can transform a disabling condition into little more than a discomfort.

Do what comes naturally and easily to you

Lastly in this section is the reminder to focus on the things that come naturally and easily to you. If an exercise feels contrived or awkward you're less likely to do it or gain anything from it. There may only be one thing here that feels at all 'right' for you – and that's fine, do just that. You will find, with time, that doing that one thing brings a better understanding of Mindfulness. It may also open doors to other ideas which you formerly rejected or to new ideas you discover by building from your own experience. I don't, personally, use all the ideas I have included here – I suspect it will be obvious which ones I most strongly relate to – but they won't be the same for you; we are all different. Again, I want to stress the importance of being creative in your approach and in designing your regime around your own needs and characteristics. All a teacher can do is lead you to a mindful experience and suggest ideas of how to move forward. We each have to make it work for us in our own way.

From Mindfulness to Love

It would be easy to assume that Mindfulness is a just a clinical reallocation of our mind to serve a new end, one that is more relaxed and aware, and indeed we could leave the story there if we wished. But my own feeling is that we risk missing a vital and inevitable sequel. I spoke in an earlier section about the neat bedding down of the layers of our life to minimise the ripples that propagate through to the present. That goal, to calm our mental landscape, is indeed worthy. But you might find there is more beyond that. What, for instance, is the point in being tranquil if nobody around you is? What I am saying is that the boundary of our work does not end in ourselves, as I hinted at in 'Human interaction' and even 'Walking in nature', we inevitably find that we need to move beyond merely us and it's love that makes that happen.

Patience

It sometimes seems that patience is the first quality from which all other solutions flow.

Typically we think of patience in relation to how we react to other people and the annoyances of everyday life. We forget that, in dealing with ourselves, we also need patience and that's often the way in which we are least patient. We are forever berating ourselves for not doing things well enough and, when we see faults in ourselves, we are too ready to criticise and too quick to demand change.

This is not merely to say that if we can be patient with this, or that, quality within ourselves then it will be less annoying and we'll have an easier time, although that is certainly true. It goes beyond that: As long as we are impatient with ourselves we are setting up barriers of internal conflict that are difficult to get beyond. In relationships between people making a demand on someone will often not get the best result but, if we soften our demand to a request, things often work out better. So it is with our impatience with ourselves. Once the demand for change is lifted understanding and resolution become possible. If we dismantle the rigid framework of our internal confrontation things will soften and internal relationships can begin again. We can then start to accept what we are, and how the world is, and see a route to how things might change.

Acceptance

Acceptance is always a necessary step towards change. As long as we are in denial of something we are unable to respond to it effectively and all we have is the hope that it will change. But, if we reject the pull of the past and future in favour of the experiences of now; if we are wholly embracing those experiences without preference, then it follows we are unconditionally accepting our present. All of it. That is a massive and challenging step but it is the goal of this mindful journey that, slowly, bit by bit, we accept everything about our present. That's not to say that we are necessarily accepting the past or the future. The past may have happened, but our relationship to it can change. The future is unknown but our anticipation of it can alter. We can make the distinction that to accept the present is not to accept any inevitability about the future. I may accept I am in pain, but I do not have to accept that it will always be so.

Pain (mental or physical) is a particularly important example, because a great deal of the burden of pain is in how we project it into our future. We accept a transitory pain easily, but once we suspect it might go on indefinitely we may become alarmed or depressed. Mindfulness separates these impressions of pain by allowing our present experience, but rejecting our mind's extrapolations. This has significant implications for pain management. If we restrict ourselves to the burden of our present experience we reduce our suffering by taking away the additional burden of what *might* happen. It also has the added implication for mental distress that to accept our distress is to begin a relationship with it and in that lies the roots of resolution (this is what we are doing in Insight work.) Greater discussion on pain management is outside the scope of this book (and my experience) but, if you are interested, there is a branch of Mindfulness called 'Mindfulness Based Pain Management'.

So when we sit with something in a way that is mindful we are accepting it, by definition, because we are not allowing the mind to roam and distract us from it. Over time we learn more about how acceptance feels and we can bring this into our everyday life. In our more objective moments we can ask ourselves if we are accepting or rejecting each of life's experiences. My own discovery was of just how much of my life I pushed away from and rejected. Yes, I was present and active, but it was like I was always in defence, or looking for something else other than what was there, in front of me. My full engagement was always compromised by some ulterior motive or agenda. Increasingly I see that, and try to move towards acceptance of everything – what can I say? It's a slow process!

I can see this might come across as rather inward looking. The healthy balance with all these processes is not to force anything, but to do the exercises and allow them to change our life in a natural, evolving way, without pressure or judgement or even desire. We are never driving change, we are facilitating it. We are not here to continually second-guess each motive, just to be curious when the opportunity arises.

Observation is part of the process, but self-criticism is not, so I now want to move on to another aspect of Mindfulness that will help restore some balance to that tendency. It is the realisation that to accept something is not a neutral stand, it is more. It is to open our hearts to it.

Opening our heart

In all our talk of objectivity there is the potential to see this as a process of distancing ourselves, like we might wish to do from something unpleasant, but it is more one of gaining perspective. As we develop a mindful insight into the world we are not dispassionate about what we see. We are interested, and we try and see things in a kindly way. Our mind's process of categorising things tends towards the judgemental (interesting, boring, good, bad). This is not mindful, because the values we use all come from our past. In dropping those values we can again allow ourselves to be interested in all the world around us in a less selective way and that interest is sustained, and enhanced, by seeing things in a positive, kind light. Our acceptance is not a shoulder shrugging, begrudging acquiescence to what is, but an embracing joy of what is. It is a feeling of gathering things closer to our heart and being more connected with our world, rather than being cynical or remote from it. This is not to say we have to contrive a great passion for all things, but simply that, in the balance, our disposition is a positive one; one which nurtures and encourages, and evolves naturally.

When we examine the things that give us pleasure in our lives it's interesting to question where the feeling of pleasure comes from. It is clearly not a quality of the object itself, because one person might get pleasure from something that someone else finds repulsive (the Marmite effect). Therefore it must be a quality we bring to the object. The pleasure comes from our ability to open our hearts to the encounter - and it is that process of opening our hearts, itself, that is pleasurable. So it could be said that the goal of a fulfilled life is not to go looking for more pleasurable things but to find ways to open our hearts to more of the things we already encounter. By that I mean all things, in our internal and external worlds, whether feelings, objects or people. Why wouldn't we open our hearts and enjoy them if we could?

Love

Having already taken the steps from Mindfulness, to acceptance, to the opening of the heart, I hope you will go the last, small, step with me and entertain the idea that Mindfulness is, in fact, love. Because when we say 'to open our heart' we surely mean 'to love'? Let's set aside the passionate turmoil of romantic love as something quite different and just allow a gentler, less loaded, use of the word. Love is not static, it is always dynamic. It is to wish well. It is the unconditional acceptance of something and the desire for it to evolve in its own way. In a world of love all things are moving in the direction they need to, willed on by each other. Is this willing forward, a contradiction to the mindful idea of being in the present? No, because we are not imagining or contriving a future we are just accepting that there inevitably is one, and allowing that future to belong solely to the object of love. So to love is to allow everything to flow forward freely, with our blessing. That is why it's dynamic, because it is accepting of change.

It is easy to see the implications to people around us and how it contradicts so many of the desires of romantic love (to own, to control). But is it applicable to our mindful objects of concentration? To apply Mindfulness to the tasks in our life is to do them with love - with *care*, we often say. When doing Mindfulness of breathing meditation, to bring love to the breath is to nurture ourselves. This is not loving our achievements, or 'bigging ourselves up' – it's loving that we are here to breathe. In Insight meditation it is crucial to approach all feelings with love; it melts the fear that traps our emotional past.

Love and Mindfulness are intertwined and implicit in one another. To fully understand one is to understand them both. This is not a trivial conclusion. It sits at the end of a long journey for the heart and mind but for now it is enough to be aware of the connection and allow it to inform and influence our approach to Mindfulness. Most importantly, we should allow it to help us to be kind, to be understanding and to be patient, and not least of all with ourselves, because all change starts with ourselves.

From Mindfulness to love

In time, Mindfulness will relax you and help you feel less driven by the internal and external forces that you didn't understand. You will feel better resourced and more able to cope, and your increased understanding of yourself will improve your understanding of others. You will be more tolerant, more patient, and kinder. In being more mindful you are changing yourself, changing your relationship to the people around you and, in your small way, changing the world. You will have moved closer to the source of love.

Mindful Reminders

- If you can, find a regular daily slot in your life for meditation or mindful exercises for 30-40mins. First thing in the morning, before others have woken up, will work well for many, but find the right time for you.

- Try a Yoga (Hatha Yoga preferred) or Tai Chi or Chi Kung (Qi Gong) course – all are Mindfulness of the body in motion.

- Do a Mindfulness course. The NHS run courses now. There are also several online courses.

- Read a book on Mindfulness to get another view - but only read, say, one a year. Reading about it is no substitute for doing it.

- Turn your mobile phone off more. Turn your computer and TV off more, allow silence.

- Eat meals mindfully, slow down to appreciate the taste and textures of food.

- Listen mindfully when people talk. Don't use that time to plan your reply; try just listening.

- Walk mindfully – be aware of your surroundings and your body. Nature is a mindful draw away from our selves. Notice the sun, wind, warmth, the change of the seasons and the sounds around you.

- Every time you walk through a door (or some other regular activity) use that as a cue to look at where your awareness has settled. Some people use an alarm set for once an hour.

- When you're in a situation where you have to wait and can't help it, e.g. a traffic queue, use that time to be mindful and relax.

- Try introducing small pauses between your activities; put one activity down before you pick the next up.

- When you are busy and the phone rings; at the first ring begin to disengage with what you are doing, at the second take a breath, at the third direct your attention to the caller, then pick up the phone.

- Take a few moments when busy to go back to the breath and put your attention low into the body.

- Ask regularly 'how do I feel now?' and sense it in your body.

- When you're doing something you don't like doing, just to get it done, slow down and take more time over it. Find a quality in it that interests you and try not to set deadlines for its completion.

- Try to do all things with love and care. Try to find a kindly interest in simple, mindful activities. Take up a craft or artwork, take care over the process, but don't worry about the result.

- Notice how much you pre-judge the future based on what has happened in the past. Give the future a chance to unfold in its own way.

- Try to find the good qualities in the present. Don't keep looking to the past or future to provide something better or more interesting.

- Always try and stay with what you *feel* about something that bothers you, rather than what you *think* about it.

- If you have a physical health concern, if you can't relax away the discomfort, then relax everything around it and let go of your thinking reaction to it.

- If you're experiencing discomfort or even pain and it's causing you distress ask yourself how much of that distress is because of the discomfort itself and how much is because you feel it shouldn't be there; that it's somehow 'not right' that you should have to feel it.

- Notice the extent to which your interface with people like shop or office staff feels like an obstacle to get beyond. Remind yourself they are people, take an interest in them, approach them in a human way.

- Try a body scan, recordings of guided body scans are available.

- Consider going on a retreat to deepen and refresh your experience of Mindfulness.

From Mindfulness to love

"Forever is composed of nows"

Emily Dickinson

Thanks to the following people:

To my wife, Stephanie, for her painstaking proof-reading and her unswerving support for my mindful life over the years.

Also to the first encouraging readers: Jan, Ian, Tamsin and Peter C.

To my mentors:

Janette, Farhat, Peter C, Celia, Penny.

Peter and everyone at The Barn/Sharpham.

Saimma, Daniel, Lesley and Fatimah at Rumi's Circle.

Rujimitra, appicha.

And then thanks to everything else.

Printed in Great Britain
by Amazon.co.uk, Ltd.,
Marston Gate.